CW00675064

ISBN: 1-4392-2537-0

Dedicated to my wife, step daughter, son and all of those who've served honorably in any branch of the United States Military.

Table of Contents

4. Camouflage
    4.1 Individual
    4.2 Equipment
    4.3 Fighting position
    4.4 Light & noise discipline
    4.5 If you don't need it, don't bring it.

5. Basic individual tactical movement techniques:
    5.1 Low crawl
    5.2 High crawl
    5.3 Bounding
    5.4 Moving with stealth
    5.5 Movement covering respective sectors:
    5.6 Shoot and move

6. Basic team or squad movement formations:
    6.1 File with lead & flanking scouts
    6.2 Line
    6.3 Wedge (Triangle)
    6.4 Modified wedge
    6.5 Diamond
    6.6 Trail team wedge

7. Basic team or squad movement techniques:
    7.1 Crossing a danger area
    7.2 Bounding over watch

Preface:

A paintball team can be as devastating on the course as an armed, trained and ready fire team of professional infantrymen. The fundamentals of paintball are not only marksmanship, but also the ability to move as a team, react to a threat and overcome the objective with force. To think quickly and effectively, and react decisively to any threat.

It's more fun to kill on this playing field than to be killed and knowing how to maneuver yourself and your team to victory are the keys to success.

This book is intended as a primer or refresher for those with little or no experience with or knowledge of modern military doctrine or infantry tactics. This handbook is by no means complete in all aspects or guarantees victory in every engagement. But this handbook will give you some insight as to the actual methods used by our and other forces in areas of the world in which real conflicts are a reality. None of this material is classified or restricted from public access, and written entirely from hands on experience and training.

Enjoy and play safe.

He, him, man etc represents either gender.

Safety:

- Always point your weapon in a safe direction or at the ground.

- Never point your weapon at anything unless you intend to destroy or paint it.

- Always follow the range or course rules and guidelines for Safe and Fair play.

- Follow the manufactures recommendations for your particular weapon.

1. Basic marksmanship:

1.1 Sights:

Become familiar with the sights on your particular weapon. It's fun to 'fire from the hip' or to pretend to be some 'cowboy gunslinger' or 'gangsta', but accuracy leads to winning. A single accurate shot is much more effective and a lot more fun than a whole container of 'full-auto' missed shots.

Most paintball guns don't have functional sights or aren't very accurate using the fixed sights combined with the ball containers location on top of the weapon where the sights should be. The paintballs themselves are often out of round or almost elliptical.

For these reasons, reliable accuracy will be very difficult or impossible to obtain. Fire a few practice shots to get a general idea of where your paintballs are going to land and adjust from there. Practice is always important.

Note the lack of sights on a typical paintball gun.

1.2 Sight Picture:

The correct sight picture will have the tip of the front sight pin in the center of the rear peep sight hole (generally located on the top rear of the receiver) or the front sight pin will be flush (flat) along the top of the rear sight 'v' groove. For further explanation, see your particular weapons owners' manual.

Breathing actually affects your shot. The rise and fall of your chest slightly changes the orientation of your weapon just enough to make you miss your target. Exhale before firing or just hold your breath, aim and fire.

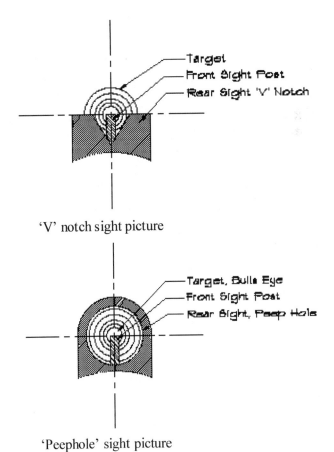

Target
Front Sight Post
Rear Sight 'V' Notch

'V' notch sight picture

Target, Bulls Eye
Front Sight Post
Rear Sight, Peep Hole

'Peephole' sight picture

1.3 Zeroing your weapon:

The best strategy is to zero your paint ball gun at 15 meters.

Fire three rounds into a target ranging from 15 meters to 25 meters away to find where your paint balls will land.   Adjust your point of aim (compensate) to hit the target or adjust your sights (recommended).   Refer to your owner's manual for your particular model and follow the manufacturers recommendations on adjusting your front and rear sights.

Do not compensate (Kentucky windage) while adjusting your sights.   A small mechanical correction may be all you need.

Always use the same point of aim while attempting to 'Zero' your paintball gun.

Use three rounds at a time for each sight correction and practice your marksmanship for a tight group of shots to ensure that your rounds will fall on target and eliminate your opponent from play.

A paintball gun with accuracy will be a challenge to all that oppose your team.

Many things may cause your paintball gun to lose it's zero. Bumping your weapon, dropping it, low Co2, playing with the sights...   They can normally be brought back, by re-zeroing your weapon.

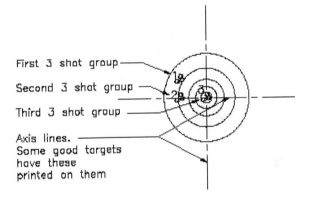

First 3 shot group
Second 3 shot group
Third 3 shot group
Axis lines.
Some good targets
have these
printed on them

Fixed Front and Adjustable Rear sights:

1. Fire a 3 shot group using the center of
the bulls eye as your point of aim.
Bring your shot group down, first to align on
axis with the bulls eye, using your oringinal
point of aim.

2. Adjust rear sight up/down per
manufacturers recomendations.
Generally, raising the rear sight post Raises
the shot group, Lowering it drops your
group. (Note) Raising your rear sight also
helps to fire from a distance.

3. Fire your second three shot group.
Adjust your rear sights side to side.
Generally, moving it to the right will bring
the group to the left.   Moving it left will
bring your group to the right.

You should be on target.   Repeat your 3
shot groups and adjust only up/down or
side to side between groups.

Adjustable Front and Rear sights:

1. Fire a 3 shot group using the center of
the bulls eye as your point of aim.
Bring your shot group down, first to align on
axis with the bulls eye, using your oringinal
point of aim.

2. Adjust front sight post per manufacturers
recomendations up/down.
Generally raising the front sight post drops
the shot group, Lowering it raises your
group.

3. Fire your second three shot group.
Adjust your rear sights.
Generally, moving it to the right will bring
the group to the left.   Moving it left will
bring your group to the right.

You should be on target.   Repeat your 3
shot groups and adjust only your front or
rear sights between groups.

For weapons without sights, practice firing at objects at different ranges to determine how much the paintball drops during distant flight and what kind of spread the shots will have. Two shots using the same point of aim could land a few feet apart at a distance. Practice, Practice, Practice.

1.4 Marksmanship:

Practice your marksmanship and drop those rounds where you want them to fall.   No more relying on luck and a ton of wasted shots...   Good marksmanship comes with patience, practice, and a huge container of paintballs...

Zero your weapon, practice the fundamentals of marksmanship and shoot with confidence that you'll hit what you're aiming for.   As the US Army Snipers say, "One shot, one kill.

1.5 'Kentucky windage':

Pick a point of aim at a tree or other object 20 feet or so away for a paintball gun, squeeze off a few shots and look at the difference between where you were aiming and where they landed. Then adjust your point of aim to where you think the paintballs will land.

For shots that a farther away, apply the principles of 'Kentucky windage' while simply aiming slightly higher to allow the paintball to arc until it makes contact with your opponents face shield.

Practice with a distant target, tree or opponent.

2. Individual firing positions:

Individual firing positions are 'reflex' positions for our combat arms soldiers, namely Infantry.   (Nothing against Armor or Artillery). These combat skills are adapted for gaming but the intent is the same. To quickly position yourself by reflex into a comfortable and steady firing position oriented towards your opponent.

These should be learned and practiced and are some of the most basic fundamentals to any combat engagement.

Even a seasoned veteran with actual combat experience is always practicing the most basic of techniques.   Both on the rifle range and in the field, even after it has become a reflex the need to stay sharp is constant.   Don't be afraid to get dirty!

2.1 Prone supported firing position:

Laying down ankles flat on the ground with your toes out, firing side knee bent. Support your weight with your elbows while resting your weapon on a sandbag, log or anything that holds your weapon in a comfortable position. Hold your cheek against the stock while looking down the sights.

It is difficult to hit someone who is lying down in the prone position. The effective target area is basically just your head and shoulders (from a distance), but that advantage is gone if they're right in front or above you. Combined with the fact that they may not expect you to be lying down, this position could be very effective, provided you have room to maneuver. But, even in close quarters paint-ball, a hit to the foot is still a hit.

Unconventional, but laying on your back may also be a very effective strategy for a close quarters one person hasty ambush, as long as you can quickly get up to change your position so that your opponent(s) cannot easily get your location or that you can effectively cover all avenues of approach. That would provide you with a new very painful hit location on your opponent.

You won't make many friends playing that way though.

2.2 Prone unsupported firing position:

Laying down ankles flat on the ground with your toes out, Firing side knee bent. Support your weight with your elbows holding your weapon at a comfortable position. Use your bones, not your muscles to steady your weapon. Hold your cheek against the stock while looking down the sights.

2.3 Kneeling firing position:

(Right handed firer) right knee down with toes flat on the ground and sitting on your right heel. Left elbow rests on left knee while steadying yourself and aiming your weapon.

A kneeling firing position reduces your profile. The hardest person to hit normally is kneeling behind a tree. Kneeling offers maneuverability and cover behind an object.

In the open, a kneeling target presents a smaller profile than standing.

2.4 Standing firing position:

Standing with weapon raised, looking down the sights.

2.5 Walking firing position:

Walking with weapon "at the ready", Raise weapon to align the sights with your target. Bend knees slightly and take slow 'sure' steps, heel to toe. Reflex sights are recommended to improve accuracy.

2.6 Close Assault, Running while firing (for suppression):

Running with weapon raised, sights aligned with target. (Good luck on hitting anything at a distance). Good for enemy suppression at medium range and close assault.

3. Sectors of fire:

3.1 Individual Sector of fire:

Your individual sector of fire is generally straight ahead or an orientation assigned to you.   Left flank, Right flank, Rear security. Prevent a "friendly" from entering your sector of fire by adjusting your sector to the left or right.

In a defensive position your sector of fire is straight ahead and 45 degrees to the left and right (90 degrees in front of you).   The sectors of fire of the fighting positions next to you on either side should overlap yours.

While moving, your sector of fire will be what is assigned, while slowly scanning from the front (to see where you're going), side (predetermined left or right) and rear.   Or to your front and each side in a sweeping motion, if you're leading the element, assuming that the rest of the team trailing you is covering the rear.

Individual tactical movement will be covered in chapter 5 Basic individual tactical movement techniques.

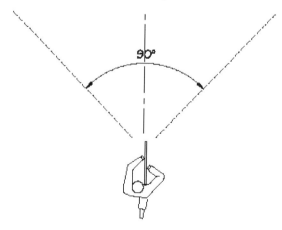

3.2 Team and Squad Sectors of fire:

The infantry squad typically consists of two Fire teams. Each fire team consists of four to six soldiers. Each squad is eight to twelve soldiers. An infantry platoon has 4 to 5 squads.

Each element moving together, typically teams or squads are responsible for their own security and their own respective sectors of fire. Within each team or squad, each individual is responsible for his or her respective sector of fire otherwise there would be blind spots within the perimeter, moving or stationary.

If the point man were to make contact and anyone were to abandon their sector, the entire element could be wiped out from a single hidden enemy sniper or flanking element. Not good. Pay attention, scan your sector. Everyone on your team relies on you to secure your sector. Stay alert, stay alive.

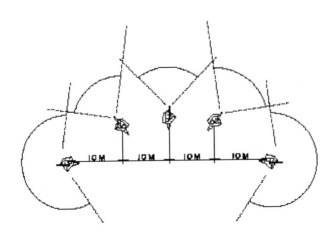

A typical Mechanized Infantry Fire Team
Author second from left

Rifleman/Dragon   Automatic Rifleman
M16A2, Dragon Missile   M249 SAW – light machinegun
    Rifle/Grenadier   **TL – Rifle/Grenadier**
M16A2 w/ M203 (231pfw,smg-dismount)   M16A2 w/ M203 & Radio
Javelin AA Missile
      M2A2 Bradley Fighting Vehicle (Background)
      25mmAC, 240C MG, TOW missile, 231pfw, Radio

Mechanized infantry (heavy) fire teams operate independently or with
armored support while dismounted.

4. Camouflage:

If he can see you, he can hit you. You must be concealed from observation and be covered from enemy fire. Camouflage yourself, your equipment and your position. Natural concealment is always best.

*Camouflage is anything you use to keep yourself and your equipment from looking like what they really are using both natural and man-made materials.

*Outlines and shadows can be broken up with camouflage.

*Movement draws attention. Stay low, move slowly, behind cover or concealment and only move when necessary.

*Improve your camouflage often. Too much camouflage can make your position obvious.

Natural Materials: Bushes, Braches, Grasses, Weeds, Shadows

Man Made Materials: Camo Paint, Soot, Burlap strips, Netting, Drab cloth strips

4.1 Individual:

Break up your outline, from your helmet, body, arms, legs to your boots. A snipers guillie suit does this effectively. Use the natural vegetation of your area or try to match it with man made materials.

Use camouflage face paint for your hands and face, or wear gloves and a full camouflaged face mask with the outline broken.

Insert twigs and lumps of grass into the gaps and straps of your uniform and equipment or create a guillie suit.

Guillie suit.
An old camouflage or military style shirt and pants with little cuts or straps to insert twigs and grass.

4.2 Equipment:

Tie drab colored burlap to your weapon and your equipment to enhance their camouflage and break up their outlines.   Avoid jamming the operating parts of your weapon or blocking the flight path of your projectile.

4.3 Fighting Position:

Make your position look like a natural part of the landscape using natural materials, grasses and foliage. Try not to locate it in and obvious place and avoid open areas. Locating your position next to trees, grasses or bushes makes camouflaging much easier as it's natural and already prepared.

Remember to hide the cut marks in trees from removing branches with a little mud or dirt to hide that fresh cut look you've added to your surroundings. Also remember to hide loose dirt under leaves.

Inspect your position from the front and sides periodically to ensure that it stays natural looking. Improve your camouflage at every opportunity.

Your camouflaged position should look as if it isn't even there. Anything you add or cut down to improve your sector of fire should appear as if it has always been that way.

Remember that too much camouflage will make your position stand out.

4.4 Light & noise discipline:

Do not leave shiny or light colored objects in view. Paint shiny equipment to prevent detection.

Do not use a flashlight or other light source during night operations. Navigate or scan using night vision devices, moon or starlight. Your eyes will adjust to low light levels.

Do not speak unless necessary. See chapter 12 for hand and arm signals for communication between team mates during silent operations.

Move silently while approaching an enemy position. See chapter 5. Basic individual tactical movement techniques for more information.

4.5 If you don't need it, don't bring it.:

Extra's on your uniform may look cool but don't always serve any practical purpose other than getting lost in the woods, giving away your position, or distracting you by the need to adjust it. If you don't need it, don't bring it.

A small assault pack is perfect for putting your gear into and a few of those cool little things that you want to show your team mates. Who knows you may actually need that cool little thingy.

5. Basic individual tactical movement techniques:

Before you attempt any form of movement,

- Conceal your movement and do not silhouette yourself. Stay low behind cover or find a low or covered and concealed route to travel through.

- Move directly and quickly from one covered or concealed position to the next without getting in front of your over watch or suppressing team or obscuring any of your teammates fields of fire.

- Scan the area for the enemy, and for your next position.

5.1 Low crawl :

The low crawl gives you the lowest silhouette possible. Use this method to cross places where cover and concealment is very low and enemy fire and observation prevents you from getting up.

Keep your body flat against the ground. With your firing hand, grasp your weapons barrel. Let your weapon rest on your forearm keeping the muzzle and receiver off the ground. Let the weapons butt drag on the ground.

To move, push your non firing arm forward and pull your firing side leg forward. Then pull with your non firing arm and push with your firing side leg, dragging your non-firing side leg. Repeat without alternating sides.

This is the slowest but safest way to move across a "danger area".

5.2 High crawl :

The high crawl is much faster than the low crawl and still allows a low silhouette. Use this technique when there is good concealment but enemy fire or observation prevents you from getting up.

Lie down supporting your upper body with your elbows and cradling your weapon in your arms keeping the muzzle off the ground. Alternately advance your right elbow and left knee and your left elbow and right knee while moving to your next fighting position.

5.3 Bounding:

Bounding or rushing is the fastest way to move from one position to another.   As a general rule, each bounding movement should last from 3 to 5 seconds.   Another name for this movement technique is the **'Three to Five second Rush'** for a reason.

Try to keep rushes short to prevent the enemy from tracking you.

Always try to bound or rush from one place of cover to another.

Never bound into the open and extend your rush should you need to reach cover.   The longer you are exposed, the easier it is to hit you.

From a laying down covered position,
Slowly raise your head, if previously undetected, to scan your next covered position.

Slowly lower your head, tuck in your arms and bend your left or right knee.
Raise your body by extending your arms.

Get up quickly and... Run to the next position.
Drop down and assume your firing position.

With a rifle you would catch your fall with the butt of the stock
and move in a forward motion with the rifle naturally going to your
firing position. You'd break your paintball gun if you did it that way.

Go to your knees and fall forward, naturally assuming your firing
position.

5.4 Moving with stealth:

Moving with stealth means moving quietly, slowly and very carefully to avoid noise and detection.

Ensure solid footing by keeping all of your weight on the foot on the ground while stepping.

Raise your moving foot high to clear branches, brush or grasses.
Gently let the moving foot down toe first, with your body's weight on your rear leg, careful to avoid twigs, loose stones and dead leaves.
Lower the heel of your moving foot after the toe is in a solid place.
Shift your body's weight and balance to the forward foot before moving the rear foot.
Take short steps to maintain your balance.

Squat down periodically behind cover to listen to the sounds of your environment and attempt to detect the presence of "enemy" contestants through their noisy and sloppy movements.

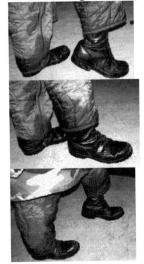

5.5 Movement covering respective sectors:

Each individual in a team, moving in any formation should be pre-assigned a sector of fire. Scanning their respective sectors, each individual should be scanning for their next position or cover, and signs of the enemy.

While scanning your particular sector of fire be sure to employ the principles of moving with stealth.

Ensure that 360 degree security is established because the enemy could have snipers or observation posts out that could easily be in a position to flank you. Looking behind you every once in a while could prevent them from winning.

Overlapping fire is recommended, but do not allow any of your team mates into your sector of fire, and do not move into someone else's sector of fire. You are keeping them from rapidly reacting to enemy fire.

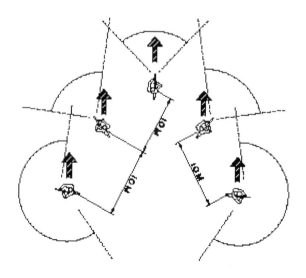

5.6 Shoot and move:

While engaging your opponents without adequate reserves on your side, be sure to change your position (move) often to ensure that they cannot bring other "enemy" forces into position or establish a flanking position. Fire a few bursts and continually advance or fall back. Keep moving; do not stay in the same place.

An American sniper during the Vietnam War destroyed an entire company (about 120) of NVA soldiers by firing one to three shots and moving to another firing position. He kept them from pinpointing his position.

Utilize an alternating firing element and moving element if operating as part of a team.

While the firing element is in position, the moving element utilizes individual movement techniques to establish a closer position to attempt to destroy the enemy or further away to establish a base of fire to cover the forward positions withdrawal in the case of "breaking contact".

In either case, one element fires while the other moves and should alternate between the moving and firing team so that the entire element stays within yelling distance or eyesight.

In an engagement, stealth and noise discipline do not apply, unless you are in a flanking element attempting to surprise the enemy.

While the firing element is in position, the moving element utilizes individual movement techniques to establish a closer position to attempt to destroy the enemy or further away to establish a base of fire to cover the forward positions withdrawal in the case of "breaking contact".

In either case, one element fires while the other moves and should alternate between the moving and firing team so that the entire element stays within yelling distance or eyesight.

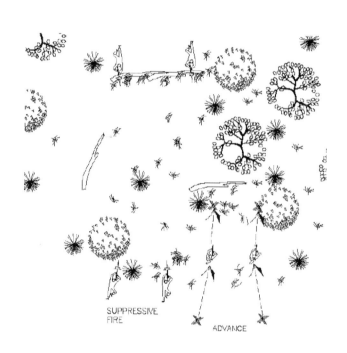

SUPPRESSIVE
FIRE

ADVANCE

6. Basic team or squad movement formations:

6.1 File with lead & flanking scouts:

Moving as a team or squad in a file or formation, the team should employ a lead or point man acting as a scout for the element. The lead man should be with-in eyesight or yelling distance to alert the rest of the element upon contact with opposing forces.

Flanking and rear scouts should travel along the sides of the file at the same distance to ensure that an enemy ambush would not hit the main element.

This formation should **not** be used while expecting enemy contact.

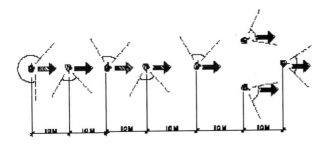

6.2 Line

Walking in line towards the objective would be used to flush out opponents and employ all available firepower onto a target to the front.

Each team member should walk side by side with 10 to 20 feet between them and drop to the ground upon contact.

This is not recommended for tactical movement.

This formation provides 100% cover to the front or rear with minimal cover to the sides.

This formation is easily spotted and flanked.

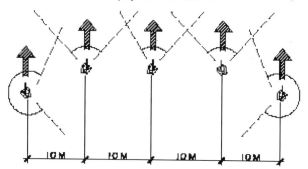

With this formations shortcomings also comes its versatility. It enables the entire formation to put the maximum available firepower to the front towards the enemy and is the standard infantry and armored combat formation for most Warsaw Pact countries.

This formation is typically deployed with units side by side to form a wide 'front' and echeloned deep. If the first few echelons get destroyed or mowed down, the following echelons move through. In WWII the Russians typically would give weapons to only the first few echelons expecting the following echelons to pick up weapons from their fallen comrades. It is rumored that the modern Chinese do the same.

6.3 Wedge:

This is the most common and very effective four to six man team sized movement technique. The strength of this technique is in the maneuverability and control it allows between the team and the team or squad leader.

The firepower of this formation can quickly be oriented to respond to threats from any direction while maximizing the abilities to search for and defend against an opposing force. Each individual is first set up in the formation and assigned a sector of fire to prevent friendly fire incidents. Security is performed by all.

The lead position is responsible for forward security while the flanking members are responsible for flank and rear security. The team or squad leader is in the middle controlling the lead mans direction of travel.

Upon engagement with an opposing force all of the team members forming the wedge formation should move on line with the man facing the enemy, and be within distance to respond to the team leaders' commands.

This formation provides 90% cover to the front or rear while providing 50% to the sides.

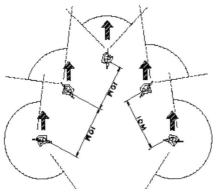

6.4 Modified wedge:

The wedge formation can be inverted or lined up heavily to one side.   These modifications to the pattern can be used in situations where contact is expected or to perform a hasty flanking maneuver with part of the squad to quickly subdue the opposition.

This formation provides 90% cover to the front, and one side or the other, while only 50%-60% to the sides.

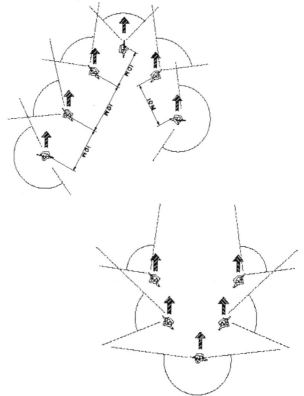

6.5 Diamond:

This is a common 4 man team sized element formation where a rear security person is required.   The benefit of this formation is also that the team member furthest from the fight can quickly move to reinforce his team, where he or she is needed most.   Additional members can also be added to form a "cigar shape" formation.

This formation provides 75% of the force ready to react to the enemy to the front, sides or rear at any time.

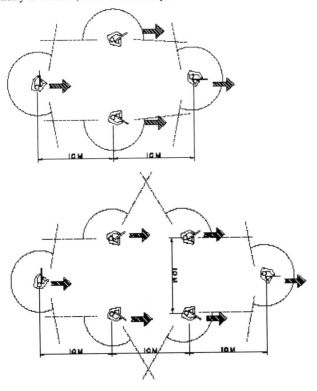

6.6 Trail team wedge:

This is used for larger elements. The trail team forms a wedge formation and can quickly respond to threats to the lead team by flanking the enemy or by getting on line and assaulting.

This formation provides 0% cover to the front, 90%to the rear while only 50%-60% to the sides.

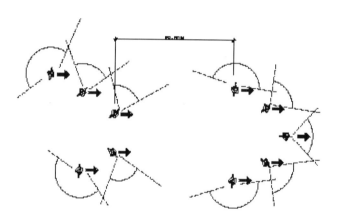

7. Basic team or squad movement techniques:

7.1 Crossing a danger area:
Danger areas such as roads, trails, streams, power line, etc. should have at least one person kneeling and covering both directions while the team moves through one person at a time.

'Scrolling the road' involves each person taking a turn at security while the element moves across the road. The second person kneels; the third person kneels behind him covering the opposite direction. The first person runs across the danger area and kneels to provide security. The third man then runs across the road to secure the opposite direction while the rest of the element moves across the danger area until the entire element has crossed.

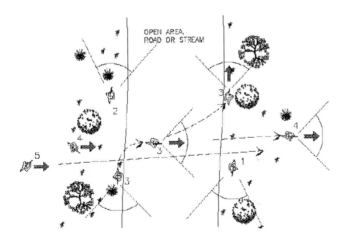

There are a million and one ways to properly execute this maneuver. Proper security must be maintained and clearing the area just beyond the danger area is also a high priority.

Fig. 7B Illustrates a simple alternative.
The First and Second people secure both directions. Three and Four cross and run opposite loops to scout a small area beyond, then take positions again covering both sides of the danger area, while the Fifth person crosses and covers the direction the element is or will be moving. Finally Persons One and Two cross. The unit regroups, reforms into their traveling formation and continues into harms way.

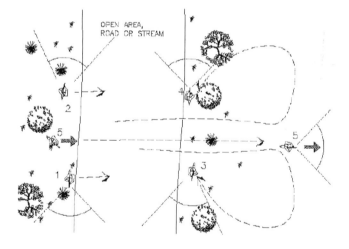

7.2 Bounding over watch

One man or team moves while the other man or team establishes a base of covering fire to keep the enemy's heads down during movement utilizing individual movement techniques. When the moving element gets into position and becomes the firing team, the other team moves beyond the firing team and into their position. Repeat until every member of your team is on line and engaging the enemy.

*See '(5) shoot and move Figure 5Q

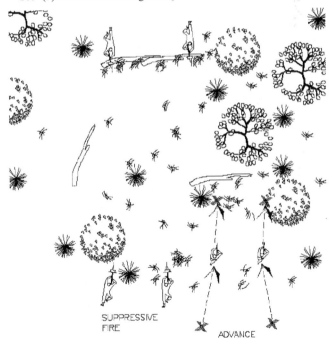

SUPPRESSIVE
FIRE

ADVANCE

8. Navigating terrain

Navigating terrain to find the enemy position while keeping yourself and your team in the best possible covered and concealed routes is the hardest part of being the assaulting force. It is best to avoid open areas, trails, and roads but sometimes it's necessary to cross these natural obstacles.

Keep to the edges of large open areas or spread out widely in a wedge formation.

'Scroll the road' for crossing roads, streambeds and trails. *See 7. Crossing a danger area.

Don't take the easy way into a wooded or any area. It could be set for an ambush or to funnel you and your team into the enemy 'kill-zone'. Go through the brush and don't worry if you tear your new cool looking 'army' pants, or get a little dirty. Deploy flanking scouts or snipers who can quickly react to contact received from the main element, or draw the main element to where the enemy is.

Avoid a file formation when expecting contact. Spread out and move from covered position to position while scanning for the enemy.

8.1 Covering Distance

If your opponents known location is far away, a File formation is the quickest way to get where you need to be.

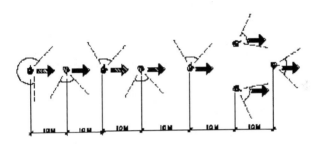

File formation employing lead and flanking scouts with rear security.

8.2 Movement to Contact

If your opponents location is unknown or within the vicinity, use a wedge or diamond formation. A spread out line formation is useful to locate or flush out the enemy position. Upon locating them, fall back to regroup, at a pre-determined rally point, plan your offensive and move into the direction of expected enemy contact utilizing one of the before mention movement techniques from Chapter 6.

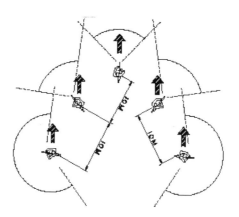

8.3 Tracking Patrol

Look for signs left by the enemy element.   Move in your assault formation with stealth.

One squad tracks while the others provide security.

Position your primary tracker to the front with security to his immediate flanks.   A wedge or diamond formation is perfect for this.

To counter tracking, disperse widely, circle back, change directions, offset your path using waterways, roads, snowdrifts, etc. Walk backwards retracing steps from an area that your tracks could get lost in, combined with circling back, you could easily confuse them.

9. React to direct fire:

9.1 React to far ambush:

Upon contact with an enemy force (with room to maneuver), Drop to the ground and move to a covered position.   Minimize your exposure to enemy fire.

Move your element on line by utilizing individual movement techniques and suppressive fire.

Once your team is on line you can begin to concentrate on fixing and suppressing or maneuvering to destroy your opponent.

9.2 Suppressive fire:

A 'base of fire' should be brought upon the enemy for suppression while elements of your team can move into position.   Fire enough to keep their heads down and sustain their suppression until your moving element can get into position and resume firing.

It is much easier to maneuver while your opponent is suppressed than dodging paintballs.

In a situation where you are suppressed, try to move or get one of your teammates to try to take out the opponent suppressing you.

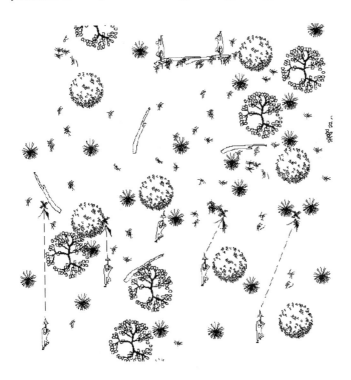

9.3 Assault the objective:

Frontal assault. Bounding by buddy teams or by fire teams onto the objective area to over-run the enemy. Each man should utilize individual movement techniques and not take unnecessary risks to achieve the objective. Do not just get up and charge if you can maneuver using individual movement techniques.

The only situation where you should charge is in a close ambush where one short rush would get you on top of your opponent, otherwise you are simply caught in their kill zone.

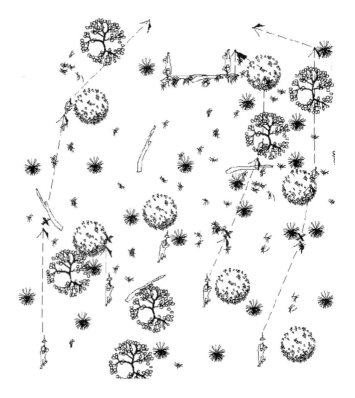

9.4 Flanking maneuvers:

With your suppressive fire team in place a second (assault) team moves to the side and out of the enemy's line of sight, around and assaults the objective from the side or rear.

Utilize stealth and individual movement techniques to surprise the enemy from the side of their position.

If you find your team is suddenly flanked, maneuver yourself or your team out of the crossfire.

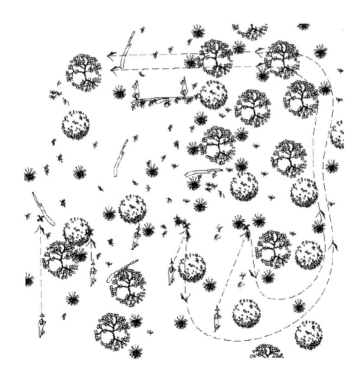

9.5 Pursuit:

Maintain formation and utilize individual movement techniques while chasing down to destroy the remaining enemy elements. Position your Fire teams on line or in a wedge formation to find, fix and destroy the enemy. Bound by teams to overrun the enemy. Repeat as required.

You do not want the enemy to fall back to their secondary positions while all of your people are just charging.

If you find yourself or your team in a situation where you are being chased. Conduct a hasty ambush. Position yourself in a concealed position. The element of surprise is the key element of any ambush.

9.6 Breaking a close Ambush:

If you are the assaulting force and you find yourself in the middle of a close ambush with no options for safely maneuvering out or away, Charge the attackers.

The Chaos of the ambush will have them concentrating on the guy in front of them. A few of you will make it through their kill zone and you'll be beside or behind them. Run along their line, slightly behind them and take them out before they take your entire team out.

10. Withdraw under fire:

Withdrawing under fire may be necessary if you encounter prepared positions with no way to destroy the enemy from your angle of approach. It may be necessary to fall back (withdraw), establish a base of fire to keep their heads down (suppression) and maneuver to re-orient yourself and your team to the objective or to move a concealed part of your team into a flanking maneuver to over-run the enemy from the side or behind.

10.1 Individual (1 person):

Get behind cover, stay low and move quickly to your next position. Go from position to position until you are out of the kill zone.

10.2 Buddy Team (2 people):

Get behind cover, stay low and move quickly to your next position. Bound as a team out of the kill zone. Move one person at a time alternating suppressing and moving from position to position until you are out of the kill zone.

10.3 Fire Team (3-5 people):

Get behind cover, stay low and move quickly to your next position. Bound by buddy teams out of the kill zone. Move two people at a time alternating suppressing and moving from position to position until your team is out of the kill zone.

10.4 Squad (2-3 Fire Teams):

Get behind cover, stay low and move quickly to your next position. Bound by buddy teams out of the kill zone. Move two people at a time alternating suppressing and moving from position to position until your entire squad is out of the kill zone.

One Fire Team moves back, by buddy teams, then the next Fire Team moves while the first suppresses the enemy. Try to have only One Buddy team moving at a time. While in contact, silence is out the window. Yell to be heard "Alpha Team One, Fall back", "Cover me while I move" and "Got you Covered", "Bravo Team One, fall back"…

Designation is for Alpha Team One = Buddy Team One (Alpha), First Fire team., Buddy Team Two (Bravo), First Fire Team. Then Alpha Team Two = Buddy Team One (Alpha), Second Fire Team, etc.

11. Defensive positions

Ideally you'd like to set up obstacles to block movement into hard to defend areas. Set up obstacles to funnel enemy movements straight to you, while you're concealed from view. Let your cleared sector of fire mimic an abandoned trail or clearing with all evidence of broken tree limbs and brush hidden or 'painted' with mud or dirt.

Overlapping sectors of fire are recommended with the space between them to seem hard to pass through, by the use of strategically placed tree limbs or branches placed to look like thick brush.

11.1   Hasty fighting positions:

A hasty fighting position can be any place you may find cover. A rock, tree, a log, anything you can hide behind to fire and conceal yourself.

By military standards a hasty firing position is a quickly prepared fighting position (Shallow graves). They are typically dug one m-16 wide by 3 m-16's long and 2 bayonets deep (18") and camouflaged to appear as a natural part of the environment from the front and sides

11.2   Prepared fighting positions:

A fighting position or bunker that can be defended from all sides would be ideal, especially if there are only a few people playing, but if you have a few people on your side and have the time to prepare a course, dig or prepare a few fighting positions, keeping in mind the rain. So you might not want to dig too much to have it all flooded the next day.   If the soil is sandy and water is dissipated quickly, A fox hole would probably be your best bet.

A simple log cabin style bunker would be perfect, especially if you provide overhead cover and can camouflage it to look natural. Simply grab some dead tree braches off the ground, a saw or hatchet and build away.   Don't forget support stakes driven into the ground and string or wire to hold everything together.   The advantage of this type is that it won't get washed out or flooded by the rain.

11.3 Secondary defensive fighting positions:

Ideally right behind and slightly elevated above your primary prepared fighting position with the same attention to overlapping fields of fire.

Set up your secondary fighting position to fall back to and positioned so that if your primary fighting position is over-run, the enemy cannot effectively use your primary position to their advantage. Leave the back of your primary bunker open with walls that come straight out towards your secondary position. You will have a prepared and secure place to fall back to if need be with easy access to you and it won't be used as effective cover for the enemy.

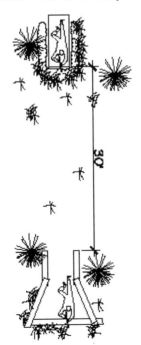

11.4 Preparing avenues of approach:

Set up obstacles to block movement in hard to defend areas or to funnel the enemy into an ambush area.

When crossing a field or moving through the woods, people tend to look for openings in the brush. These opening can be natural or appear natural. By removing or placing thick vegetation, you can direct their movement to where you want them to go.

In open woods, placing deadfall and a loose pile of natural looking branches can achieve the same affect. Be careful so as not to build them a hasty fighting position by providing cover and concealment.

Find a way to discourage the enemy from using any potential fighting position. An animal carcass, old bones or dog, deer or rabbit feces, even a plastic snake or mouse could make good deterrents and distractions.

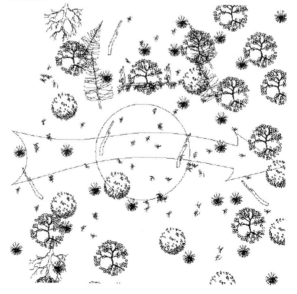

11.5 The art of ambush: Deliberate Ambush

Ambushes make up one of two types of combat patrols. The first is a raid (assault), second, an ambush.

There are two categories of ambushes, Deliberate and Hasty.

There are also two types of ambushes, point or area

Finally there is the formation employed in the ambush. Lineal or 'L' shaped, or any modification of the two based on time or terrain. There area a million ways to properly execute an ambush and often time available or terrain will dictate how your team is laid out. Be prepared to modify your plan according to the situation.

The element of surprise is the critical element of any category or type of ambush. Setting up an ambush in any environment is not as hard as it may seem. There are many factors in your favor. Cover and concealment is usually abundant in any environment or terrain. The real key to success is to select an ambush site that severely limits your opponent's ability to maneuver out of your kill zone or to find and hide behind cover.

Set your people in a concealed defensive position and hold your fire until all of your opponents are in your kill zone.

The priority of fires would be their leading, trailing and especially flanking elements.

Wait until they are close to your position without detecting you. Close proximity will limit their ability to maneuver, but also limits their options to close assault, or panic and run.

Ideally, they would be stuck in your kill zone and wiped out.

Deliberate Ambush

An Ambush is a surprise attack from a concealed position.

Select an obvious avenue of approach such as a stream bed, trail, Road, Field, etc. Anyplace that the terrain will direct the enemy movement or the most likely route is an avenue of approach. Select hasty fighting positions or prepare your fighting positions along the ambush site.

It is recommended to fall or move dead trees, brush etc. to direct the enemy movement. Create a barrier that will unknowingly direct your 'enemy' right into your field of fire. But be careful not to provide them with cover or concealment.

Stringing an obvious piece of wire or rope at 3 feet above the ground will do the job and they probably wouldn't think twice about it as long as it appears old, like it has always been there. Just lean trigs on it to make it stand out as a barrier, being careful not to provide cover or concealment for them.

Assign pre-determined sectors of fire to your team members and hold your fire until the enemy is within effective range and within your 'kill-zone'. If you are properly camouflaged, they could literally step on you without realizing that you are even there. Special Forces and Snipers train to use small bits of natural vegetation over a large area to completely cover themselves. Step on them and they still don't move. They exercise extreme patience until you are in their kill zone.

When the enemy is in sight, wait until they are all in front of you and coordinate your firing. Take out the biggest threats along with the enemy flanking elements first. Pick off targets inward from the flanks or those closest to you.

If they know you are in the area and they walk too far away without finding you, don't let them know where you are and compromise your position. They'll come back and probably give you an opportunity to annihilate them. They'll likely be frustrated by not finding you the first time and become lax and unorganized.

Your ambush should be able to withstand an assault from the front and sides. Lay out your men in an arc shape with an extra man, your team leader, to serve as rear security and reserve.

If they do have to turn around to find you, ensure that you won't have to move much to respond to a different direction of attack. A small adjustment in your orientation should be all that you need to do.

Allow scouts to pass through the kill zone or take them out if it's an easy shot, without alerting the main element. Move 'dead' scouts out of the area after their out of the game by motioning for them to lie or sit down somewhere, preferably out of sight.

Try not to initiate the ambush while your opponents are too far out. Distance gives more options for maneuverability. Try to wait until the whole group is right in front of you, initiate fire to pin them down and destroy them. As they used say, "wait until you can see the white of their eyes".

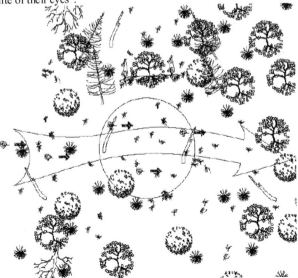

A Hasty Ambush allows no time for preparation. You see the enemy and get into a rough lineal pattern of hasty fighting positions, quickly and quietly. Use hand and arm signals to communicate. Post security elements to cover your flanks.

Variations on the age-old ambush.
L shaped ambush. Position your men in a large L shape with appropriate security. The element facing the flank of the enemy conducts an assault on the enemy forces while the main ambush element, positioned laterally facing the enemy picks them apart. The Main element adjusts fire when the assault element approaches to cross the front. For paint ball, get up and join the assault!

Area Ambush:
Position a central ambush with smaller flanking ambush sites that can both assault the enemy flanks from opposite directions. (For paintball only, grunt). The real deal, the smaller flanking ambushes lie in wait for retreating enemy forces, but you already knew that.

12. Scanning (See them before they see you)

Scanning your sector of fire is the most important activity that you do while waiting for the enemy to show up. See them before they can see you. While moving and in the defense.

The Fundamentals of Scanning.

You are looking for anything that does not appear natural.

* Sounds of movement

* Shiny objects

* Obvious tracks or trails

* Color Contrast

* Outlines or Shadows

* People moving

12.1 Scanning while in the Defense

Quickly scan your entire sector.

Scan each piece of your sector starting with the area closest to you; go from side to side, then up and down, paying attention to anything that is not natural.   Scan to the maximum distance you can see, paying close attention to anything that catches your eye. A spotting scope makes this a lot easier.

12.2 Scanning while moving

Move slowly scanning 50 to 100 feet away while moving. Pause behind cover often to scan and listen.   It's better to spot them while their still out of range than to be caught in a close ambush.

Typically you would scan from the front to the sides and behind you.   Don't be afraid to assume rear security.

13. Infantry Hand and Arm signals

Seeing a hand and arm signal you should make eye contact with the person behind you and repeat the hand and arm signal so that everyone knows what is going on. (These hand and arm signals build confidence and cohesion in moving silently as a group and also reinforces the effectiveness in the use of hand and arm signals). Be open to make up and improvise new or different hand and arm signals. Go over each of them so that everyone knows what each of them mean.

During the actual engagement, yell to be heard. Silence is no longer necessary.

As soon as the threat is destroyed, immediately return to stealth. Moving and communicating quickly and silently.

* **Assign a Sector** – Chopping motion to each side of you bending at the elbow at 45 degrees to your left and right, or what ever sector you want covered.

* **Bounding over watch, (by squad)** – Similar to Bound by teams but with flat hand. symbolizing one squad moves while the other squad covers. Flat hand, then roll your arms like you're pedaling.

* **Bound by teams** – two fingers up with one hand, then rolling your arms, like pedaling.

* **Cover me** – Finger extended up with palm of other hand over it.

* **Danger area ahead** – Open palm down, slash across your chest diagonally.

* **Double time (RUN)** – Pump arm over your head

* **Enemy in sight** – hand extended like an upside down pistol

* **Flank Left** – Extend left arm out like a one arm hug, while extending finger pointing in direction of travel.

* **Flank Right** - Extend right arm out like a one arm hug, while extending finger pointing in direction of travel.

* **Follow me** – With your arm extended behind you with your palms up and open, bring your arm over your head in a wide arc.

Formations

* **Diamond formation** – Put your hands together to form a diamond.

* **File Formation** – Chopping motion behind you.

* **Line formation** – Both Arms out to your side in a chopping motion, if you are in the middle, otherwise one arm in the direction you want everyone to go.

* **Staggered File Formation** – Chopping motion staggered, chop to one side then the other like making an 'x' (while moving).

* **Wedge Formation** – Two fingers extended horizontal, similar to peace sign with palm facing downward.

* **Group together** – With your hands open, motion like you're pushing two objects together.

* **Halt** – Fist above your head.

* **Head count** – Pat the top of your head, Each man quietly counts to let the leader know how many people are available, or if anyone got left behind.

* **Leader, 1 Sqd** – Shake your collar and hold up 1 finger.

* **Leader, 2 Sqd** – Shake your collar and hold up 2 fingers.

* **Move in that direction** – point in direction of travel.

* **Move with stealth** – Slow walking fingers over open hand.

* **Quiet** – One finger to your lips.

* **Rally Point** – Rotate hand over head then point to an area designated to fall back to.

* **Scan your sector** – Point to eyes then out, side to side.

* **Scroll the road** – Tap your shoulder then roll one hand down your arm.

* **Security** – Point to your eyes with two fingers from one hand.

* **Traveling Security/Scout to the front** – Point to your eyes with two fingers on one hand, Then Put your hands together then open them moving away from you towards the direction of travel. Chop with far hand. Point to direction of travel.

* **Traveling Security/Scout to the side** – Point to your eyes with one hand, Then Put your hands together opening them to the side away from you in the direction you want to post security. Slide hand (back to front) with far hand to your side, Chop and point to direction of travel.

* **Spread out** – With the backs of your hands together, open them like you're pushing two objects apart.

* **Team 1** – One finger raised.

* **Team 2** – Two fingers raised.

* **Withdraw** – Backward chop while extending one finger towards direction to move to.

Hand and arm signals should be adapted or modified to your team. Discuss what signals your team should add modify or use.   Ensure that every member of your team is aware of what each one means and what actions they should take when they see it.

The lack of illustrations enables each team to communicate the same thing differently.   Enabling a silent 'code' understood only by your team.

14 Concepts of war:
These concepts are based upon common military practices and procedures.

14.1 American Military:

American doctrine is loose and allows the field commanders the ability to easily adapt to any situation. Given the specific objective for the mission, codes of conduct, ideals, humanitarian and political issues. The commander can establish the plan of action while minimizing casualties and collateral damage.

Wars are not won by our machines and weapons but by the soldiers, sailors, and airmen who use them. Pinpoint accuracy, training and efficiency, ready to engage and destroy any enemy, on any battlefield terrain. Even the best equipped army cannot expect to survive on the battlefield without trained and motivated soldiers, inspired by their competent leaders.

Superior training and equipment will bring our fighting men and women to victory.

Destroy objective 'A' while distracting or misleading objective 'B' with a smaller force. Initiate contact, overrun objective 'A' and reorganize. Repeat for objective 'B'.

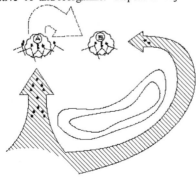

14.2   Former Soviet Union Military (Warsaw Pact):

Soviet doctrine is rigid to the letter of any given plan.

Tactical success leads to the goal of operational and strategic success. Massive fire, maneuver and violent strikes make up the "operational art" of soviet doctrine. Utilize surprise and extreme, overwhelming exertion of coordinated force with all available means at the enemy's weakest point to dominate the battlefield.

Attack unexpectedly and swiftly in echeloned mass, over-run the enemy relentlessly and disperse immediately after the tactical or operational goal has been achieved with little regard to losses.

Destroy objective 'A' before moving on to objective 'B' in force, bypassing strong points. Aggressive recon, followed by a rapid and decisive assault to

Combat formations are echeloned deeply with narrow fronts and stick to 3 distinct forms of maneuver.
1. Frontal attack utilizing echelons,
2. Flank attack,
3. Enveloping attack to surround or force the enemy to turn and fight in a new direction, abandoning or making prepared positions ineffective.

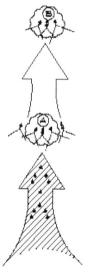

14.3 Insurgent and terror tactics:

There is no place in paint ball for suicide tactics unless you strap paint can to yourself. Or you could easily say that the unorganized and sloppy "enemy" are the insurgents. Similar to guerrilla tactics.

14.4 Guerrilla warfare:

Characterized by small unit hit and run tactics. Contact (violent ambush) and withdraw to a secondary position to regroup, refit and re-organize. Opportunistic attacks without adequate reserves.

Sounds a lot like paintball…

15. Glossary of terms

Ambush: A surprise attack on the enemy as they pass through an area.

Avenue of approach: The most likely route that the enemy will approach from.

Bound(ing): Moving as a buddy team, fire team or squad where ½ of the element moves while the other ½ is in position and covers your movement by scanning for or suppressing the enemy.

Combat operations: Any part of planning, moving, preparing for or engaging the enemy.

Concealment: Anything that you can hide behind that obscures sight but does not block shots.

Cover: Anything that you can hide behind that blocks shots.

Doctrine: Rules established by your government or unit.

Engagement: Firing at the enemy, locked in combat.

Fire team: 3-6 people or soldiers operating as a team.

Flank: Attack from the side or rear of the enemy element.

Hasty: Quick unprepared position.

In Force: All available men and equipment.

Light Infantry: Soldiers whose primary job is to fight on foot, without the benefit or support from vehicles.

Marksmanship: The ability to hit what you're aiming for, utilizing the fundamentals of shooting.

Objective: Any place where the enemy combatant(s) are set up to defend or a key piece of terrain.

Obstacles: Any thing that blocks or hinders movement or sight through an area.

OP : Observation Post: Placed in front of to the side of the main element to observe enemy movement. Very effective with a radio. Can be used to lead the enemy into an ambush by making contact and falling back or deliberately getting their attention at a distance.

Over watch: Security, scanning for the enemy, while a team moves.

Pursuit: Chasing the enemy.

Sector of fire: The areas that you are responsible for scanning for the enemy.

Sight picture: The alignment of your front and rear sights, or the sight through your scope.

Suppressive fire: Firing just enough to keep the enemy's heads down without an opportunity for them to return fire or observe your movements.

Zero: Adjustment of your sights so that your rounds or paintballs hit what you're aiming for. It may be necessary to elevate your sight picture for further shots taking into account the drop of your paint balls over a distance as long as the rounds land straight onto what you're aiming for without sideway movement.

References:
STP 21-1-SMCT Warrior Skills Level 1, Dec. 2007,
Approved for public release

FM 7-8 Infantry Rifle Platoon and Squad, April 1992,
Approved for public release

NOTES:

NOTES:

2679709

Made in the USA